www.facebook.com/notebooktown

Shop our other notebooks at
notebooktown.com

This Book Belongs To

SCHOOL BUS

PRIVATE CAR

COLOR THE CAR

TAXI CAR

POLICE CAR

COLOR THE CAR

AMBULANCE

COLOR THE CAR

TRUCK

SCHOOL BUS

COLOR THE CAR

BUS

CYCLE

COLOR THE CAR

MOTORCYCLE

COLOR THE CAR

CRANE

COLOR THE CAR

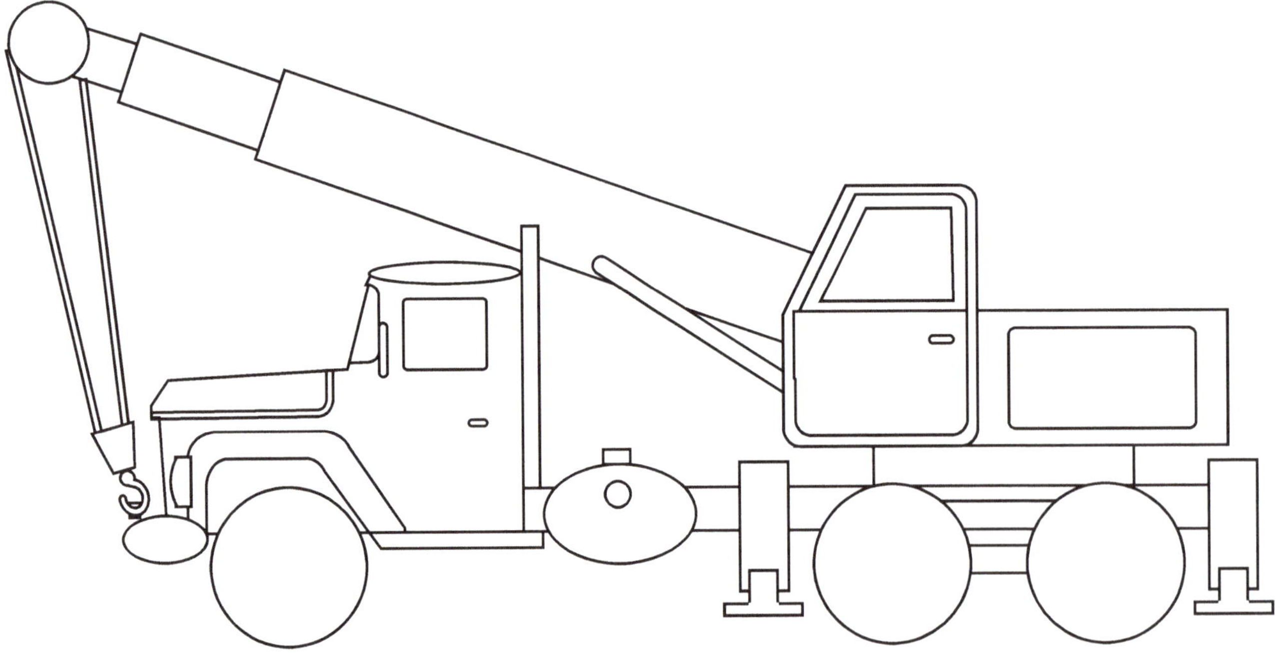

PRIVATE CAR

COLOR THE CAR

CRANE

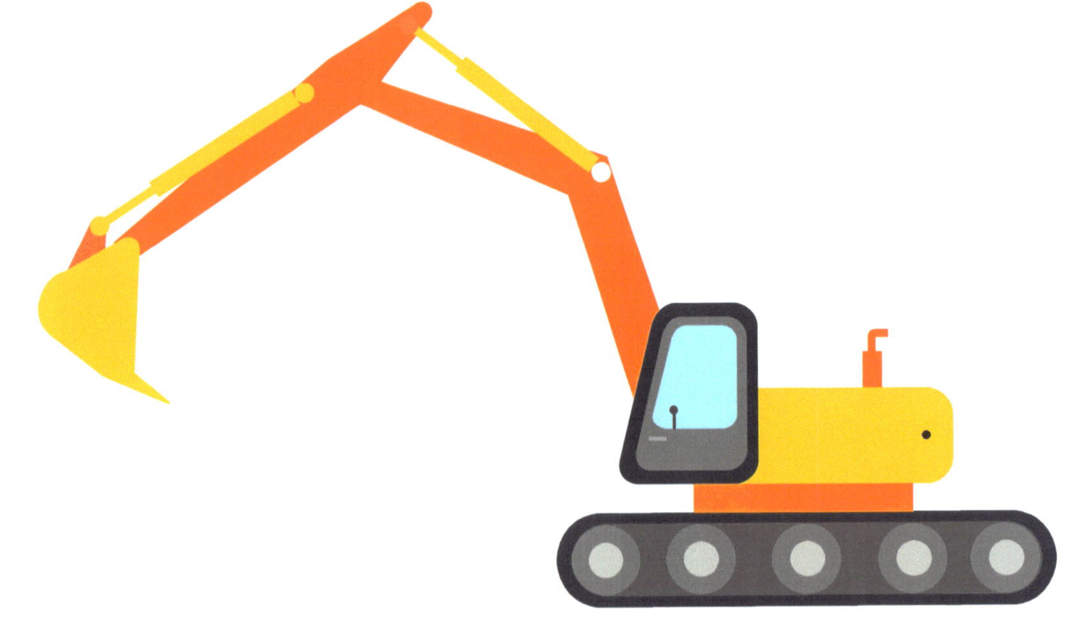

COLOR THE CAR

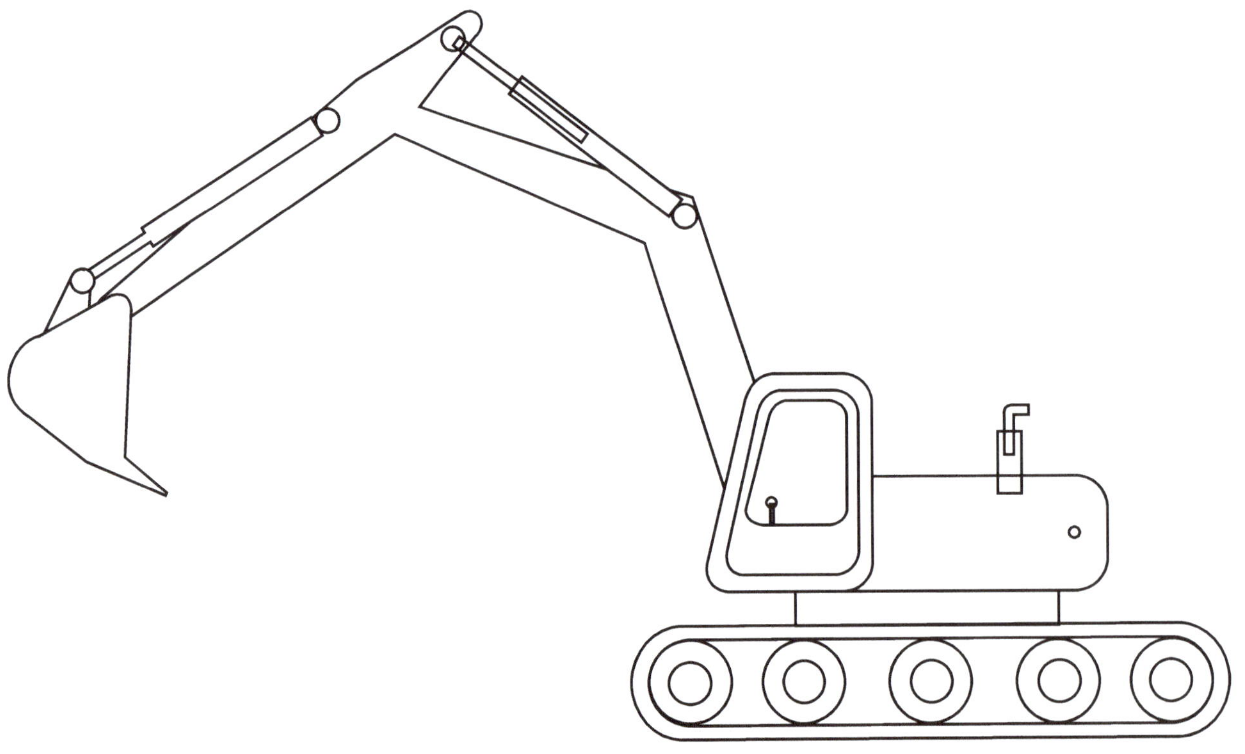

TRAIN

COLOR THE CAR

MIXER TRUCK

COLOR THE CAR

BULLDOZER

COLOR THE CAR

TRUCK

COLOR THE CAR

BUS

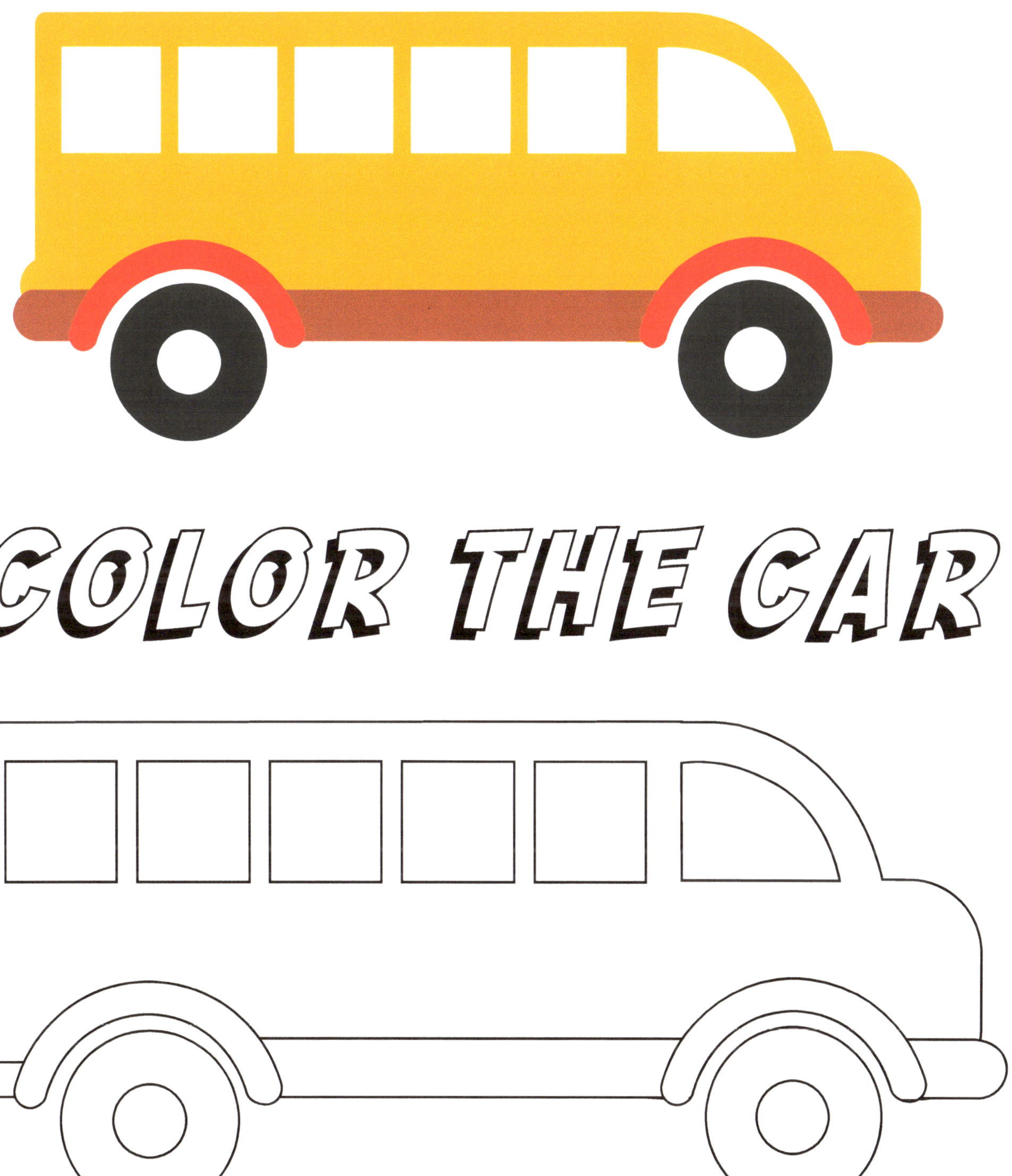

COLOR THE CAR

ROLLER

COLOR THE CAR

DUMP TRUCK

COLOR THE CAR

TRUCK

COLOR THE CAR

TRAIN